C0-AWC-740

Giuseppe Ungaretti

by GLAUCO CAMBON

Columbia University Press
NEW YORK & LONDON 1967

Giuseppe Ungaretti is Number 30 of the series

GLAUCO CAMBON is Professor of Comparative Literature and Romance Languages at Rutgers University and Fellow of the Indiana School of Letters. He is the author of *Recent American Poetry*, *The Inclusive Flame*, *La Lotta con Proteo*.

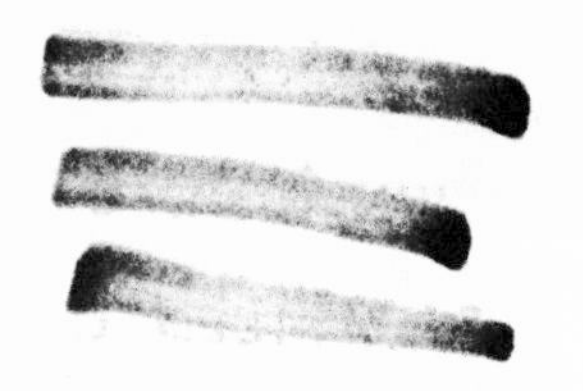

Library of Congress Catalog Card Number: 67-27359
Printed in the United States of America

Grateful acknowledgment is made to Giuseppe Ungaretti and to Mondadori Publishers of Milan for permission to quote, both in the original Italian and in my translation, from Ungaretti's work, *Vita d'un Uomo*.

Giuseppe Ungaretti

The Egyptian city of Alexandria enjoys the unique distinction of having given Europe two of its finest modern poets: Giuseppe Ungaretti and Constantine Cavafy. It was not so strange for the Greek Cavafy to be born in the city which had been for centuries the center of Hellenistic culture and was still harboring a thriving Greek colony. It was incongruous instead for Ungaretti, patriarch of modern Italian poetry, to be born in Alexandria and to spend there the first twenty years of his life. On that stormy night of February 10, 1888, when he came into the world, his working-class parents—Tuscan immigrants both—could hardly have dreamed of the exceptional literary future which was in store for their newborn son. Obviously, the wind of poetry "bloweth where it listeth," and any reader of Ungaretti's autobiographical pages in the collected travel memoirs, *Il Deserto e Dopo* (*The Desert and After*), can see for himself how providential this peculiar destiny turned out to be for our poet.

The pattern that emerges from Ungaretti's life is one and the same thing with the unfolding of his literary career. The element of chance marking his improbable beginnings will be converted into spiritual necessity at the end, so that nobody now could imagine modern Italian poetry without Ungaretti, and Ungaretti himself without his remote African birth. What might have been a hopeless handicap—his coming into the world and growing up in a place so utterly alien to Italian culture and not even peripheral to the Italian linguistic area—became a unique asset. It impelled him to seek, on many levels, the "promised land" of his fathers. *La Terra Promessa* (*The Promised Land*) is in fact the title of his volume of verse published in 1950, but above all it is a myth pervading his poetry from the very start. In poems like "Popolo" ("People," in his first book, 1916), "1914–1915" (in his second volume, 1933), "Terra" ("Earth-Motherland," in his third book, 1947), the Promised Land appears as Italy, the land which "finally spoke/to the son of emigrants/. . . with the fatal grace of millennia." On a more symbolic level, in the 1950 *Terra Promessa* sequence the myth takes the shape of the never-never land which has lured Aeneas away from forsaken Dido, and which Aeneas' pilot, Palinurus, will never reach. Throughout our poet's work, the inner quest for "an innocent country" persists beyond any geographic reference. Finally, it is the Italian tradition as embodied in the smooth verse of Petrarch, Foscolo, and Leopardi that has relentlessly attracted foreign-born Ungaretti. The promised land of a poet is the timeless poetry which will sustain and liberate him, a tradition rediscovered.

Thus the myth of a Promised Land has shaped Ungaretti's poetry as a quest for roots, for fulfillment, innocence, and form; and he owes the poignancy of that quest to the accident of birth which placed him in the predicament of a prodigal son of Italian culture. This is, so to speak, his "negative" debt to Egypt and Alexandria, while a specifically positive one must be seen in the colorful Arabic folklore, in the voluptuous fantasy and biblical desert vision that haunt his verse as a counterpoint to the Promised Land myth. Time and again Alexandria rises in the horizon of a poem as the fairyland city which was both native and foreign:

I saw you, Alexandria,
Friable on your ghostly foundations
Become sheer memory to me
In a suspended embrace of lights

. . .

I am of another blood and never lost you,
But in that loneliness of a ship
Sadder than usual there came back
The regret that you, foreign, should be
My native city.

These lines are from "1914–1915," a poem written in 1932 and included in *Sentimento del Tempo* (*Feeling of Time*, 1933). Elsewhere the poet remembers Alexandria's minarets "garlanded with lights," or the ceremonies of its labyrinthine Jewish quarter, or the whole white city in the consuming embrace of the sun, vanishing aft:

From the white-painted
ship
I saw my city
disappear,

and a Thousand-and-One-Nights spell will be cast on him:

In the eye
of Thousand-and-one-nights
I have rested

In the abandoned gardens
she was alighting
like a dove

Both quotations are from Ungaretti's first book. In a later poem, written in 1924 and called "Ricordo d'Affrica" (Memory of Africa), the desert-born mirage will be Diana, goddess of light, suddenly appearing in the palm clumps "between the endless plain/and the wide sea . . ."

But the 1916 poem, "In memoria" (Memorial), penned at a village on the Italian front during World War I, embodies Ungaretti's African background as an excruciating experience of exile, not as delectable mirage. Mohammed Sheab, his Egyptian fellow-student who killed himself in Paris because he could no longer be an Arab and had no homeland left, haunts Ungaretti as a reminder of what it means to lose one's roots. For Ungaretti too sees himself as a nomad. In poem after poem he envisages the lure and the curse of a wandering life:

In no part
of the earth
can I
make my home

Thus "Girovago" ("Wanderer"), of 1918. It is this autobiographical persona that links in one imaginative experience the two poles of Ungaretti's world: Desert and Promised Land, memory and hope, loss and fulfillment. As late as 1960 he wrote:

One roams the desert with remains
Of an earlier image in one's mind,
Of the Promised Land
Nothing else is known to the living.

His work therefore develops through the several stages of an ever-renewed quest which is as personal as any confession can be and yet transcends the merely personal. The poet himself has said, of his early volume now retitled *L'Allegria* (*Mirth*), that

This old book is a diary. The author has no other ambition, and he believes that even the great poets had no other, than to leave a fine autobiography . . . form worries him only because he wants it attuned to the variations of his spirit, and, if he has any progress to show as artist, he would like it to point also to some perfection he has attained as man.

And he has clinched the point by naming the entire sequence

of his published works *Vita d'un Uomo* (*Life of a Man*). Yet, in the introductory note to the 1960 book called *Il Taccuino del Vecchio* (*Notebook of an Old Man*), he says that, though most of the verse therein took its cue from very personal events, these "motifs . . . should no longer count as the author's own in the work, if he has managed to give it the life of poetry."

If so, poetry is to Ungaretti neither what it was for Eliot (an "escape from personality") nor what it had been, in Eliot's opinion, for generations of Romantics (an effusive "expression of personality"), but a search for the archetypal meaning of personal experience. This makes his essential biography directly relevant to his work, where he neither hides nor imposes his own self, but questions it to look for revelations that will outstrip the merely private sphere. (The significance of his poetical "diary" is further enhanced by the involvement with crucial experiences of modern history, climaxing in two world wars.) We have already seen what it meant for Ungaretti to be born in Egypt to parents of peasant origin from Tuscan Lucca (his father was drawn to Egypt by the demand for foreign workers which Ismail Pasha's government had created with its great public-works projects). Along with the exotic Moslem elements described in the initial chapters of *Il Deserto e Dopo*, the growing Italian boy absorbed from Alexandria the suggestions of remotest history and certain vital contacts with modern French culture, which had made itself felt in Egypt ever since Napoleon's time. Two French brothers with important positions, Henri and Jean Thuile, befriended young Ungaretti and opened their rare library to him.

French was a second language to him almost from the start, if we consider that he attended a French school in Alexandria, while Italian remained his mother tongue, the language of the home, also heard in the diaspora of workers about town, with the languid melody of Arabic impinging from the background. For the rest of his wandering life Ungaretti would carry this in his memory—Alexandria and its chorus of tongues, its gardens on the edge of desert and sea, its submerged Pharaonic seaport which was to provide a symbolic title for his earliest booklet, *Il Porto Sepolto* (*The Submerged Seaport*). Since French culture, so germane to Italian and so blessed with prestige, had always been close to bilingual Ungaretti, it was logical for him to sail for France in 1912 and spend the next three years in Paris, attending the courses of Henri Bergson and other luminaries at the Sorbonne.

But his Parisian education, to be sure, was not confined to University classrooms. Those were the years when the artistic revolution stirring all over Europe found its main focus in the French capital, which afforded a haven to restless talents of every nationality. Here were the Fauvists headed by Matisse, Vlaminck, and Vuillard, the Cubists Picasso, Léger, Braque, and Gris, the Futurists loudly advertised by Marinetti, also born in Alexandria; here Gide developed his omnivorous consciousness, and here gravitated Expressionism from beyond the Rhine, Imagism from beyond the Channel. . . . In such a thrilling atmosphere Ungaretti found all the stimulation he needed. He met practically every major figure in the artistic world of the cosmopolitan capital, and struck up a friendship with Guillaume Apollinaire, the Italian-born French poet of Polish extraction who was superseding the cultist heritage of *symbolisme* with his Whitmanesque poetics of directness, modernism, and free analogy. To hear Ungaretti talk of his long-dead friend today, one hardly realizes that almost half a century has elapsed since Apollinaire died in 1918. They had respectively enlisted in the French and in the Italian army, and if the author of

Alcools and *Calligrammes* did not physically survive the war, it was lucky that Ungaretti at least should be spared, for unlike Apollinaire he was just at the beginning of his literary career.

Apollinaire too was a restless exile in search of a homeland (he obtained French citizenship while serving in the army), and in him Ungaretti could sense a brother. The parallelism between Ungaretti's early experiments in verse and Apollinaire's own ventures is certainly a marked one. Both poets modernized diction, simplified syntax, and abolished punctuation, to give a sense of suspended flow to their free rhythm, with the consequence that their vivid imagery stood out the better. One recalls the analogous attempts of their contemporary William Carlos Williams, also a visitor to Paris before and after World War I. But Ungaretti's debt to his colorful fellow poet, amply acknowledged by himself and documented by Luciano Rebay and G. Sempoux, is no passive borrowing. Beyond the technical affinities one can always hear each poet's unmistakable voice.

One of Apollinaire's war poems, "A l'Italie," is a passionate plea for Italy's joining the struggle on the French side in the name of a common Latin culture, and it is dedicated to Ardengo Soffici, the Futurist writer and painter from Florence who had been doing so much to foster the vogue of avant-garde French art in his native country. Around the café tables of Montparnasse, Soffici, Papini (another Florentine iconoclast), Apollinaire, and Ungaretti had a chance to discuss their dreams of creative revolt. And it was Papini and Soffici's magazine *Lacerba* that published Ungaretti's first poems in January 1915. *Lacerba* was competing with Prezzolini's *La Voce* for the role of Italian rallying center for new writers and revolutionary thinkers; *La Voce* had initiated Ungaretti to modern Italian culture during his Egyptian days. Paris, and Apollinaire's friendship in particular, were for Ungaretti an integral phase of his cultural formation and yet, at the same time, a way station to his Italian motherland.

Italy's entry in the war on the Allied side in May 1915 induced Ungaretti to volunteer for the Italian front against the Hapsburg Empire. It was there, in the stony Carso region of the Eastern Alps, that he jotted down several of his best poems, flashes of insight bursting through the shell of established prosodic convention to capture the immediacy of inner experience. Wireless imagination, he called it, in the wake of his fellow-Alexandrian Marinetti. Meanwhile, he strove to keep in touch with the war-shattered republic of letters. As providential chance had it, help came in an unforeseen way from Lieutenant Ettore Serra, who one day recognized in a withdrawn buck private the author of certain promising pieces he had read in a Florentine avant-garde magazine. Ettore Serra promptly saw to it that Ungaretti's new sheaf of poems, the harvest of the trenches, would be collected in book form. This way *Il Porto Sepolto* (*The Submerged Seaport*) was privately printed at Udine in the neighborhood of the front lines. Somehow the limited edition (80 copies) found its way to a number of responsive readers, thereby obtaining for the young soldier-poet important recommendations that made it possible in 1919 for him to secure an influential publisher (Vallecchi of Florence) and a larger audience. A new edition, enriched by an additional section which gave its title to the whole book, *Allegria di Naufragi* (*Mirth of Shipwrecks*), led to Ungaretti's recognition as the foremost poet of the new generation.

One powerful reason for this early success was, along with the radically innovative style, the unrhetorical approach to the formidable theme of the moment: mass war. As against Gabriele d'Annunzio's heroic myth in which war affords a chance for superhuman gestures, Ungaretti's poetical persona embodies the intense awareness of man's existential precariousness in the face of impending death; and he interprets the military predicament as the shared burden of countless men whose anonymity is acknowledged in his own:

> Eccovi un uomo
> uniforme
>
> Eccovi un'anima
> deserta
> uno specchio impassibile . . .
>
> (Here is a uniform
> man
>
> Here is a desert
> soul
> an impassible mirror . . .)

This is the beginning of a poem appropriately called "Distacco" ("Detachment"), in which the opening line may ironically echo the *Ecce Homo* of Christian liturgy. But anonymity is redeemed in brotherhood, as the poem "'Fratelli" ("Brothers") emphasizes with its simple question—a question ideally addressed to any of the forgotten myriads that marched to their deaths in whatever drab uniforms on those trench-furrowed, shell-scarred battlefields of Europe:

> What is your regiment
> brothers?

Then again in "Peso" ("Weight") the poet opposes his own "lonely" and "bare" soul "without mirages" to the "peasant" soldier who "entrusts himself to the medal/of Saint Anthony/ and goes in lightness," for the poet does carry the weight of his own disabused modern consciousness which sets him apart from his simpler fellow-soldiers. Yet fellow-men they are, and in a haiku-like poem like "Soldati" ("Soldiers") he will express this common bond by comparing their (and his) lot to that of leaves clinging to their trees in fall.

Or he may, in "In dormiveglia" ("Half awake"), compound the sense of violence and animal fear in the image of men "huddled/in the trenches/like snails in their shells," until by a sudden reversal of the imagination the insistent rattle of rifle fire will bring back to him the familiar noise of (Lucchese) stonecutters feverishly hammering away at the lava cobblestones of his streets, while he listens to them "unseeing/half asleep." And to the "cold," "hard," "dry," "refractory," "totally soulless" stone of a war-beaten mountain he compares his own "unseen" suffering as a creature ("Sono una creatura," "I Am a Creature"). If the closeness of death makes him feel close to so many unknown men in the hour of danger, it also immerses him in an alternately dehumanizing and regenerating involvement with the elements:

Lurking in ambush
in these entrails
of rubble
for hours on end
have I dragged
my carcass
worn out by mud
like a shoe sole
or like a seed
of hawthorn . . .

That is the first part of a "Pilgrimage" which climaxes in the return to the sense of menaced, separate consciousness, while elsewhere the self is effused in the fleeting phenomena of the cosmos (see "Annientamento," "Annihilation") or takes stock of its own history in the communion of sanctifying elements ("I Fiumi," "The Rivers"), or grasps the analogy between outer destruction and inner grief in the shell-torn village of San

Martino del Carso. In the poem by that name, the poet's own heart is "the most tortured village" where "no cross is missing."

As a war poet, Ungaretti joins the company of Guillaume Apollinaire, Charles Péguy, Wilfred Owen, Ernst Stadler, and August Stramm, blown to the four winds by the wasteful fury of the conflict whose horror and pity they uttered in their several tongues.

Unlike them, he survived, and thus had a chance to develop beyond his dramatic literary initiation, but even if he hadn't there is no doubt that both as a whole and in the sampled excellence of pieces like 'The Rivers" Ungaretti's first contribution to Italian poetry would have sufficed to recommend his name to future generations. He would have been the Wilfred Owen of Italian letters, a voice cut short too soon but not to be forgotten. As happened, he found himself confronting the responsibility of his great promise in the changing climate of the postwar years. The excitement of war was subsiding into an uneasy peace fraught with unsolved problems; war-weary Italy, like other countries that had been weakened by the awful effort, teetered for a few years between Communist revolution and the old parliamentary system, then settled into the compulsory order of Mussolini's Fascist regime. Art outgrew the turbulence of Boccioni's prewar Futurism to freeze into the eerie magic of Carrà's and De Chirico's "metaphysical" painting, where manikins populated abstract spaces or empty piazzas yawned. Then it passed to the "Novecento" style—a kind of classicist modernism with academic overtones. Literature lost the buoyant revolutionary temper of the old *La Voce* and *Lacerba* days; while Marinetti's impresario-like vociferousness became a harmless institution, the magazine *La Ronda* (*The Patrol*) spread the word of a new classical style, in the austere name of Leopardi. By and large, despite the iconoclastic experiments of Pirandello on the stage, the prevalent tone was now one of introspective restraint. Ungaretti's growth as a writer after *Allegria di Naufragi* (1919) can be partly understood within this context of restoration.

There is no reason, however, to subordinate deterministically his personal literary development to the quasi-official esthetics of the time in his new-found country of origin, or to the political vicissitudes which fostered it. After all, he did not passively register a cultural climate, but rather contributed to it signally, and while the Neo-Symbolist movement of "Hermetic" poetry took shape around his work (and Montale's) in the twenties, he also aroused sharp dissent in some quarters. Croce, the most authoritative figure of modern Italian culture, rejected his poetry as an artificial distillation; Gramsci, the radical thinker, slighted him along with the whole of Hermeticism as irrelevant to the cultural needs of the time; the critic Flora, three years after the publication of Ungaretti's *Sentimento del Tempo* (*The Feeling of Time*, 1933), attacked his elliptical diction as too mannered; the charge of obscurity was often echoed. Now that Ungaretti's poetry has long ceased to be controversial, we can look back on the polemics of those two decades between the world wars as part of the new ordeal through which his art had to assert itself.

After a few years in Paris (following the transfer of his regiment to the French front in 1918) he had settled in Rome with his French wife in 1921. Before returning to Italy, he had published in Paris a French edition of his selected verse, partly self-translated and partly written directly in French: *La Guerre* (1919). He never lost touch with the world of French letters and art, where he could count on the support of such friends as Jean Paulhan. We have seen what a powerful stimulation had come to his early work from the liberating example of his friend

Apollinaire. But Rimbaud, along with Baudelaire, had also acted as a ferment from the start, and now Mallarmé, the very Mallarmé against whose esoteric abstraction Apollinaire had reacted for the sake of an open utterance, came to be increasingly felt in Ungaretti's poetics. To a large extent, however, Mallarmé's influence (to use a discredited word) blends into that of Petrarch and Leopardi. Ungaretti had reached Italy by way of France. And if it was on the Italian battlefields that he fully "recognized" himself as creature (to quote from "The Rivers"), the parallel self-recognition as poet had to come, in due time, from the ancestral master of stylistic perfection: melodious, inward-looking Petrarch, the fountainhead of a European lyrical tradition that had lasted for centuries.

Ungaretti, the initial outsider, was in the ideal situation of being able to come to the Italian tradition on his own. What others, raised on native soil, could take for granted, he never did, with the consequence that his growing attraction to the Petrarchan model of self-contained melody was no less a personal discovery than the metric freedom of his beginning phase had been. The freely repossessed tradition, while exquisitely Italian, was also broadly European, and Ungaretti remained immune from whatever complacent provincialism the nationalistic age might have encouraged. He discovered Petrarch through Mallarmé, and working with the great tradition for him was ceaseless experiment. *Poésie pure*, fin de siècle *Symbolisme*, led him all the way back to a remote poetry of timeless purity. Thus we see, once again, the providential pattern: his circuitous itinerary was a cultural homecoming, and the homeland's literature in turn needed him, the foreign born, to restore on a new basis the continuity it had lost.

One way for Ungaretti to root himself more firmly in his Italian homeland was to contribute actively to literary journals and literary sections of the daily press. His literary journalism includes essays on Petrarch and Leopardi or on versification. It took a broader shape between 1931 and 1934, when he sent articles as a foreign correspondent to the Turin daily, *La Gazzetta di Torino*, from his revisited native Egypt, from Corsica, from Holland, and from several parts of Italy, especially the Southern and central areas. These articles, now collected in book form as *Il Deserto e Dopo* (*The Desert and After*, 1961), clearly transcend journalism to the point of becoming autobiographical prose of mythic range. The poet speaks at every turn; essential phases of his inner development are recapitulated (with the exception of the French one), and motifs like the myth of Italy as Promised Land, to be later developed in books of verse in the fifties and sixties, make themselves clearly heard. In other words, these trips to sundry countries and regions are part of Ungaretti's "self-recognition."

The last part of *Il Deserto e Dopo*, which consists of translations from the folk poetry and art verse of Brazil, reflects his experience in that country, where he held the chair of Italian literature at the University of São Paulo from 1936 to 1942. The poetical fruits of those years, years marked by sorrow (the loss of his little son Antonietto) as well as by a renewed contact with the exotic nature Ungaretti's nomadic instinct seems recurrently to need, were to appear in 1947 in a book titled *Il Dolore* (*Grief*), which couples private bereavement with the shared grief of the Italian people and of mankind at large in the bewildering predicament of World War II. In 1942 the Italian government had invited Ungaretti to occupy a chair of Italian literature at Rome University. The offer was motivated by the poet's "bright fame" (*chiara fama*), and he accepted it, to hold the post until his retirement in 1962. If the circumstances of the appointment were exceptional, there were no political strings attached to it, and this was implicitly recognized by the postwar Italian governments, which never revoked it. Nor did Ungaretti take it as a sinecure. A number of students have attested to the effectiveness of his eloquence from the chair, and those who have heard his course on Leopardi at Columbia University in the spring semester of 1964 likewise remember his passionate delivery. The poet put all of himself into his teaching. Meanwhile, outside the classroom another audience had begun to respond to Ungaretti's voice in America, particularly since Allen Mandelbaum made a representative choice of his verse available to American readers in 1958. Poets like Robert Lowell, Galway Kinnell, and Anthony Hecht translated some of Ungaretti's work as part of their own poetical experience, proving once again that the energy of significant poetry can be contagious.

Our poet's vitality indeed has something remarkable about it, and it shows in his conversation as well as in the unrelenting rhythm of his work. During the more than twenty years that have elapsed since the end of World War II, *Il Dolore* was followed by *La Terra Promessa* (*The Promised Land*, 1950), *Un Grido e Paesaggi* (*A Cry and Landscapes*, 1952), *Il Taccuino del Vecchio* (*The Notebook of an Old Man*, 1960), *Il Deserto e Dopo* (*The Desert and After*, 1961), and by a number of verse translations, from Shakespeare, Góngora, and Racine, with the latest addition to date being a rich anthology of versions from Blake: *Visioni di William Blake* (*Visions of William Blake*, 1965). Some of these volumes, which since 1942 have been appearing as a special series called *Vita d'un Uomo* (*Life of a Man*), are the result of long work begun in the thirties, and needless to say, the translations are integral to Ungaretti's original poetry as part of his stylistic experience; they are all self-recognitions, like the landscapes of three continents so poignantly assembled in *The Desert and After*. At this writing (December 1966–January 1967), more volumes of *Life of a Man* are expected: Aeneas' "choruses" (perhaps to complement those of Dido and the sestina of Palinurus in *The Promised Land*) and the course on Leopardi, reduced to essay form.

Lives of the poets no longer find favor with most modern criticism, but with Ungaretti the "life of the man" is so inextricably intertwined with that of the artist that a biographical survey like the one I have been sketching seemed as good an introduction to the poetry as any. It exhibits patterns of growth and recurrence that can hardly be ignored in a consideration of the work. I have already touched on the relevance of Ungaretti's geographic and cultural pilgrimage to the nomad persona so prominent throughout his verse, and to his complementary myth of a Promised Land.

The persona and the myth are two basic constants of Ungaretti's imagination, mirroring a uniquely mobile personal history, and broadening its scope to more than personal significance. But the constancy to be expected of poetical images is not a matter of hard-and-fast identity. Such images are mythic projections of experience and they partake of experience's own protean richness; they could hardly do justice to it if they were to constrain it into stiff abstractions. Thus we find that Ungaretti's correlated mythical images, the nomad figure and the Promised Land, reappear from beginning to end in ever-changing shapes of vision and meaning, and even their correlation shifts as the emphasis alternately falls on the individual, communal, terrene, or ultramundane nature of the Promised Land, on its historical availability or transcendence, on the fulfillment, finality, or hopelessness of the wanderer's quest, whatever historical garb he may don. Much in the same way, a leitmotiv changes yet remains recognizably the same through its manifold appearances in the course of a musical score. As the constancy of a theme through its musical metamorphoses is stressed by the cyclical recurrence it may have, in a human existence or in a civilization there can be cycles of historical recurrence, and these in turn will find expression in the world of art and thought. Ungaretti's existential situation—the longing of uprooted man for valid roots—has undergone its cycles as he found and lost and found his home again; in keeping with this cyclical pattern, the theme of a Promised Land has unfolded through several metamorphoses in the course of his poetry, which parallels the stages of personal, as well as cultural, experience. In a way, Ungaretti had reached his Promised Land already in 1916, when during a brief lull in the fighting on the Italian front he could say of that rocky terrain and of the Isonzo water which kept washing away so much blood,

Questo è l'Isonzo
e qui meglio
mi sono riconosciuto
una docile fibra
dell'universo

(This is the Isonzo
and here better
have I recognized myself
a responsive fiber
of the universe),

and the meaning was both geographic, the Isonzo being Italy's Jordan, and spiritual, a matter of harmony with the living universe in the enhancing presence of death. What man desecrates with his wars, the elements reconsecrate.

But the Promised Land is periodically lost and reattained, and each time in a different way. In the decades between the two wars, as chiefly represented by *Sentimento del Tempo*, Africa itself often becomes, in the wizardry of memory, something like a Promised Land, though with the uncertainty of mirage; a lost country. Another aspect of the Promised Land is, throughout *L'Allegria* and *Sentimento*, the lost Eden of childhood ("I seek an innocent/country"). It will reappear personified in the fleeting, doomed grace of the poet's child in the strongest poem of *Il Dolore*, "Tu ti spezzasti" ("You Shattered"). In the same collection, "Defunti su Montagne" ("The Dead on Mountains") seems to indicate a haven of hope in Masaccio's religious art. Art, tradition, memory as such appear as a refuge, a Promised Land, especially in Rome occupied by the German troops and harrowed by the signs of an internecine war. But memory, as "Caino" ("Cain") forcefully states in *Sentimento del Tempo*, is also guilt and torment. Death can then be a release, thus a final haven, a Promised Land (see "Inno alla Morte," "Hymn to Death," in *Sentimento* and "La morte meditata," "Meditations on Death," in the same book). Yet "Terra" ("Motherland–Mother Earth") in *Il Dolore* anchors us to its undying promise, which is that of a life-giving civilization.

The cycle has repeated itself for Ungaretti with the return to Italy in 1942. Another war was waiting for him there, a much more cruel one to witness than the 1914–1918 one in which he had taken part as a young soldier on both Italian and French soil. *Allegria*, the paradoxical "mirth of shipwrecks," had been possible then, but now only grief, *Il Dolore*, could speak. The two titles mirror each other; the "feeling of time" has intervened to age the persona, now tried by manifold bereavements. One does "go home again," to one's people, to one's memories, to begin all over. It is and it is not the same. The new cycle is not so much a repetition of as a variation on the theme.

Yet there is a recurrence after all; the voice has redescended from the rarefactions of the first part of *Sentimento del Tempo* to a directness already obvious in that book's "Hymns," especially "La Pietà," which, unlike so much earlier and later Ungaretti, hearkens back to the knotty cadences of Jacopone da Todi, the mediaeval religious poet, rather than to Petrarch's distilled elegance. This is certainly true of most of *Il Dolore* despite the unavoidable traces of Petrarchan-Mallarmean obliquity; for it is as if the poet here touched earth again, to find once more the immediacy of *L'Allegria*, though in another key. There is more explicitness than in the first book, and a louder tone. After that phase of self-renewal, the trajectory from immediacy to stylistic abstraction resumes, to come to a head in the consummate Petrarchism of *La Terra Promessa*, where the poet ties himself to the most exacting of closed prosodic forms, the canzone and the sestina. Nothing so formal had developed yet in *Sentimento del Tempo;* the *Terra Promessa* is Petrarch with a vengeance. When partial overlappings of composition are taken into account (since the first cue for *La Terra Promessa* came from the early thirties), the cyclical pattern still emerges unmistakably. It will be re-echoed in the stylistic oscillations to follow, from the narrative explicitness of *Un Grido e Paesaggi* (especially the introductory biographical recapitulation called "Monologhetto," "Little Monologue") to the *Terra Promessa*-like manner of *Il Taccuino del Vecchio* in 1960. Concomitantly, the persona renews its arrivals and departures, the last glimpse of the Promised Land being of Mount Sinai, through a desert the living cannot hope to negotiate in their ceaseless wandering. As the persona said in "Il Capitano," ("The Captain," from *Sentimento del Tempo*), this poet is still "ready for all departures."

Ungaretti has ripened without stagnating. The kind of

Petrarchan classicism into which he has increasingly tended to reshape his style is the conquest of a tireless experimenter and not a matter of acquiescence to the literary past. This will be even clearer if we bear in mind that the peculiarly Petrarchan stylization of absence and memory has alternated in Ungaretti with a Jacoponic (and very modern) convulsiveness, to the point where, at times, smooth melodic rhythm and stressed syncopation enhance each other contrapuntally in the same poem. Chorus XIV of *La Terra Promessa* may be one salient illustration of this, with its staccato lines working as a foil to the more regularly fluent ones. Also, Petrarch himself has often been seen by Ungaretti through the baroque reflector of Góngora, while Shakespeare's sonnets and Racine's tragedy have appealed to him avowedly in the same way—as examples of baroque style in the Petrarchan tradition. Certainly one aspect of Ungaretti's approach to Petrarch is comparable to Prokofiev's treatment of eighteenth-century music in *The Classical Symphony;* one would use the term "parody" in this connection if one could strip it of its deflating implications.

Ungaretti's modernity is cogently expressed by his "individual talent" 's relationship to "tradition," to say it with Eliot. The significance of his long search for a disciplining form which could both condense and release his riotous imagination emerges by contrast from the groping quality of his first known attempts, which date from the early Paris days and are now collected (along with the many variants to poems of his first two books) in *Poesie Disperse* (*Uncollected Poems*), with an important preface by the former *La Voce* critic de Robertis. The earliest of these poems are Ungaretti's prehistory, and they show him posturing as an imp à la Palazzeschi, the genial Tuscan futurist who, before maturing into one of the considerable authors of Italian fiction, long amused himself by venting alternately his comically perverse and his sentimental moods in free verse. In his sentimental vignettes, Palazzeschi is much more the *Crepuscolare* (one of the so-called "twilight" poets in a muted, quotidian, nostalgic vein who formed a school of some importance in those years) than the tough Futurist to whom, according to Marinetti's Paris *Manifesto* of 1909, all such delicate attitudes should be bane. While in the course of his subsequent development Ungaretti was to drop the defiant comicality to be seen in some of his apprentice work, Palazzeschian sentimentality proved harder to shed, and one can sometimes notice that the process of strengthening compression many of his lyrics underwent through assiduous revisions leads precisely from that kind of "crepuscular" abandon to a terser diction.

A case in point is "Noia" ("Tedium"), whose final version in *L'Allegria* consists of seven lines strategically lopped off from the twenty that composed the original draft, now given as an independent poem of the same title in *Poesie Disperse.* In the longer version, the persona gesticulates sentimentally and comments freely on the scene ("To whom can I donate/a drop of tears/of hypocritical humanity/At the mercy of life . . ."). The clipped version looks like a casual notebook entry; actually, it has reached its proper form by being pruned of excess comment and of all emotional references to the speaker. The speaking "I" is now present only once, as a contemplative function ("I look at the heads of coachmen/nodding"), and everything is sharply focussed on the few objects (the streetcar wires projecting their swaying shadows on the wet asphalt) that suffice to evoke a melancholy urban night. The drama of the self has been objectified, and all comment, impersonally yet very poignantly, has shrunk to the resigned initial statement: "This night too will pass away." But that in turn is echoed and prolonged, as time concretely felt in Bergsonian fashion, in the final verb which concludes the poem without a period: "tentennare," "to nod," predicated of the drowsy coachmen. This nodding, likewise, parallels the swaying of streetcar wires in the previous three lines. The poem thus composes itself in two informal tercets, preceded by the meditative gesture which encompasses the whole, and its parallel structure is reinforced by paratactic syntax, utterly conformable to the unliterary vocabulary and simplified grammar Ungaretti favors in this phase so well stimulated by Apollinaire's example. Other traits which concur to the success of the poem were there from the start, especially the network of alliterative sounds gathering the seven lines into a hidden harmony; but in extracting his pearl from the mother shell, Ungaretti has also polished it. He has changed the comically descriptive "faccioni dei brumisti" (big ruddy faces of the coachmen) into the sober and more distant "teste" (heads); on the other hand, he has retained the Milanese dialectal colloquialism "brumisti" for "coachmen" to particularize his scene; and he has eliminated the three lines which followed the coachmen stanza in the original version, both because they brought the obtrusive "I" back and because they obstructed the free flow of felt duration in which the infinitive verb "tentennare" resolves the final version. The lines are unmetrical, yet the third one is an effortless hendecasyllable with a swaying effect. This, too, is typical of the *Allegria* phase, which does away with traditional prosody and with punctuation as a whole to achieve an effect of slow, transfixed speech, but without getting totally rid of the hendecasyllable because, as Ungaretti later came to feel, it constitutes the natural cadence of the Italian language. It thus can quite unobtrusively emerge in the midst of shorter, uncadenced, sometimes extremely short lines.

The technical procedure described here applies to many other poems and may well typify Ungaretti's quest for essentialness, sometimes manifested in the extreme concision of certain poems which aroused no end of both hostile and approving response. In some poems the process of structural and stylistic purification went so far as to split off one initial poem into two different ones; thus, "Chiaroscuro" is a chip off the original block of "In memoria" (which now heads the section *Il Porto Sepolto* of *L'Allegria*). "Chiaroscuro" is centered on the impressions of the contemplating self through a night of intense memory, while the pruned version of "In memoria" is focussed on the dramatis persona Mohammed Sheab; and if one takes the trouble of checking it with the initial draft, one will find that much sentimental affectation has been dropped to the advantage of the epitaph-like poem. Likewise, the poem "Levante" ("Near East"), whose original draft appears now under the title "Nebbia" ("Fog") in *Poesie Disperse*, underwent several transformations to attain the arabesque-like agility of its final form, in which Ungaretti experiments with onomatopoeia and imagery in such a way as to suggest the piercing sinuosities of Arab music and the voluptuousness of Oriental poetry. What was a disorderly accumulation of subjective imagery has become a winding gracefulness, without impoverishment. The persona no longer imposes with his redundant confessions, he simply objectifies himself as "a young man" standing "towards the stem, alone" to contrast the noisy merriment of dancing Syrian emigrants astern. Their "shrill arabesques" of clarinet music, clapping of hands, and tapping of feet evoke in him the contrapuntal vision of Jewish funerals in his hometown of Alexandria which he is now leaving behind: on Saturday nights they wind silently with their lights after the hearse through the maze of alleys. The sea, "ashen," "quivers sweet restless/like a pigeon." At the end the persona identifies himself as the observer by introducing the verb "odo" ("I hear"), with the whole previous scene as its object, while his consciousness is on the verge of "sleep." He is thus both inside and outside the poem, actor as well as spectator. Comparison with the initial version will show that again, as in "Noia," the poet has practiced faultless surgery.

So Ungaretti purged in his own development the various rhetoric (whether of the obstreperous or of the languid kind) which was in the air. Yet attentive perusal of *L'Allegria* indicates that some of d'Annunzio's sensualism, for instance, has filtered into the leaner diction of Ungaretti, while the Futurist plea for unconventional imagery, free utterance, and modernist topics has found in his controlled energy a truer fulfillment than was possible to Marinetti's centrifugal pyrotechnics of "parole in libertà" (words at liberty). Who can deny the stark modernism of the following image in "Perché?" ("Why?"), a typical war poem:

Si è appiattito
come una rotaia
il mio cuore in ascoltazione

(It has flattened itself out
like a railroad track
my listening heart)

It would be equally hard to miss the d'Annunzian note in "Transfiguration," where the persona, resting from trench warfare, feels himself reborn, feels himself to be "in the children's faces/like a pink fruit/glowing/among the stripped trees"; or in "Giugno" ("June"), where the Oriental beauty he dreams of in his night of distress is fondled by his imagination as a "panther" and appeals to him with all the sweetness of her "tar black" eyes and "gold-brown skin." But these are assimilated elements of his own experience, not literary echoes. He makes generally good use of the freedom which Marinetti noisily wastes and d'Annunzio, for all his lavish genius, often squanders. Both the mechanical and the erotic imagery are sharply focussed, and correlated to the pensive existential self. This is why, as the critic Anceschi has remarked, Ungaretti's poetry relies so heavily on elliptical analogy.

This is not to say that he always succeeds. There are, even in the revised edition of *L'Allegria*, instances of overstrained baroque analogy. Then the "fuse of the imagination" (as Emily Dickinson would have called it) misfires and the poem sounds utterly contrived, "Attrito" ("Attrition") being an example. There are also cases of cloying mannerism, like the whole first part of "Annientamento" ("Annihilation"), a poem which, after some unnecessary talk of plucked daisies, chirping crickets, and "modulated" heart, does redeem its incongruous beginning on a powerful note of cosmic effusion shading into death. These are the faults the critic Flora resented and unduly magnified in 1936 at the expense of Ungaretti's very substantial accomplishment; an accomplishment made possible precisely by that process of elliptical reduction which, despite its occasional byproduct of shrilly telescoped images, resulted on the whole in exciting discoveries of vision and sound. Like Emily Dickinson, whose imagistic epiphanies often strikingly anticipate his experiments, Ungaretti's real talent is centripetal, to the point of occasionally compressing a whole world of vision to one or two ecstatic lines, like the much discussed

M'illumino
d'immenso

(I am illumined
with immensity)

or the equally famous "D'altri diluvi una colomba ascolto"

("I listen to a dove from other deluges," from *Sentimento del Tempo*).

These are thresholds where the poet is about to leave vision and poetry itself for a mystical silence that yawns within and around his utterance, so strongly dependent is it on resonant pauses; but thresholds they are, rather than normative examples, even if we want to emphasize the haiku-like tendencies of Ungaretti. At the other end of his range we have the controlled effusion of nondiscursive narratives, such as the already mentioned "I Fiumi" ("The Rivers"), where the autobiographical "I" recapitulates the formative stages of his own history as identified with the Egyptian Nile, scene of his birth and adolescence, the Parisian Seine, the place of his tumultuous initiation to art and virility, the Tuscan Serchio, "from which two millennia perhaps/of [his] farming ancestors drew water," and the Alpine Isonzo, marking his present initiation to fullest awareness of life and death in a homecoming to the ancestral land and to the elements themselves:

> Questi sono i miei fiumi
> contati nell'Isonzo
>
> (These are my rivers
> counted in the Isonzo).

This, in the ordeal of war, is the locus of "self-recognition," which culminates the previous stations of the persona's existential pilgrimage: the prenatal memories, the "burning unconsciousness" of adolescence in Africa, the "self-knowledge" out of first manhood's chaotic experiences in the Seine's "turbid" waters. The river image becomes the archetypal pattern of the whole poem, in Bergsonian key, as often happens with Ungaretti, whose most characteristic poems tend to be experiential processes involving the self in the dimension of inner time rather than sheer timeless moments of insight. The climate of the poem is sacramental, and the persona paradoxically celebrates his "mirth" (*Allegria*) in the presence of probable death, through an act of communion with the elements; he is a "Bedouin" who huddles near his "war-soiled clothes" to "receive/the sun," after walking on water "like an acrobat" (of the Christlike variety) and resting "like a relic" in the same water, while "the Isonzo/flowing/smoothed [him]/as a stone of its own." A baptismal ceremony is enacted, with clear implications of death and resurrection.

The work of stylistic sharpening mirrors the purification of the existential self which these poems celebrate, and we can read them as a "diary," a comprehensive book, while dwelling more eagerly on those pages which best express the author's singular powers, whether these be the arresting imagery, often synaesthetically hovering between the visual, auditory and tactile-kinetic fields, or the searching use of vowel patterns in poems that renounce ostensible rhyme, or the candor itself of utterance which tends to focus on individual words. War is both felt in its tragic cruelty and transcended in a kind of Franciscan "perfetta letizia" (perfect mirth, therefore *Allegria* in a way).

The postwar volume, *Sentimento del Tempo*, resumes and develops certain main features of the wartime poetry. The Bergsonian title coherently expresses the theme and inner form of most of the poems, which often revolve on the experience of time as an inner cycle: day and night encompassing the arc of a whole life ("O Notte," "O Night"), the four phases of day ("Paesaggio," "Landscape"), the four seasons as phases of earth and of the soul ("Stagioni," "Seasons"), the climactic season of summer, the elusive magic of dawn or evening, or autumn. This was implicit in the structure of *L'Allegria*'s verse, which emphasized temporal process as an inward development resulting not infrequently in a sense of mythic time. Enhanced inwardness, however, now makes for more abstract language, and while the individual word is still fruitfully stressed, it no longer tends to stand by itself in the isolating emphasis typical of so many minimal length lines from the previous phase. Punctuation reappears. The lines now gravitate toward traditional metric shape. The vocabulary includes those literary words *L'Allegria* had deliberately rejected in its effort to break with the academic convention, and the style moves from the earlier syntactic simplicity toward complex structures of clause subordination. Petrarch looms on the horizon, absence involves the persona who had been so expressively "present" in the wartime book, and the mythical perceptions achieved there without erudite reference now seek embodiment in classical mythology: Juno, Cronos, Apollo, Diana, Penelope, Olympus.

To be sure, these are no hoary clichés but evocations. Diana "clothed in light" springs from the remembered Egyptian oasis; Juno is woman in her carnal power; Apollo is the diffuse presence of light in the open skies; Aphrodite emerges unnamed from the Ligurian Sea, a metamorphosis of the elements which the poem captures in the fleeting play of color and light. The "End of Cronos" is an intangible event having to do with the abolition of measured time in the spellbound consciousness:

> Innumerable Penelopes, stars,
>
> The Lord embraces you again!
>
> (Ah, blindness!
> Avalanche of nights . . .)
>
> And offers Olympus again,
> Eternal flower of sleep.

This mood of rapturous contemplation between memory and dream engenders its own myths, like those of "Alla Noia"

("To Ennui") and "Isola" ("Island"), which verge on hallucination, yet owe their success to the crystalline quality of diction. Here evocative magic reaches a threshold. The language itself is stylized to an extent beyond which only the volumes of the fifties will go. While the play on "phonic values," as Alfredo Gargiulo called them in his pioneering preface to the 1933 edition of *Sentimento del Tempo*, continues along the lines set forth in *L'Allegria*, rhetorical stylization on the whole has gone a long way from that book, indeed has reversed its central direction.

At this point the poet breaks through the cocoon of his own cherished mirages to reattain, beyond what threatened to become a mere manner, dramatic utterance. We thus have the second part of *Sentimento del Tempo*, called "Inni" ("Hymns"), which neatly offsets the first. The simplest way to describe the transition is to call it a passage from evocation to invocation. It is as if "pure poetry" were no longer enough, and the poet were accordingly reverting to the naked existential self of the wartime poems. The persona that savored the exquisite poisons of ennui ("Alla Noia") or caressed the mirage of Aphrodite ("Silenzio in Liguria"), or descended into the bewitched maze of his own dream ("Isola"), now desperately confronts existence with ultimate questions ("La Pietà"). The pleasures of imagination are shattered; what is wanted is an assurance of meaning, and if the poet was king in his own realm of evanescent artifacts, now he asks whether he has "torn apart heart and mind/to fall a slave to words," and he acknowledges that he "reigns over phantoms." The crisis of poetry is also the crisis of mankind at large: the persona speaks out of his own wounded isolation, but speaks also for his fellow men, whose choragus he becomes, in the course of the poem, before God—the persistently silent addressee of the impassioned utterance.

God might be only a dream, yet men refuse to surrender it. His silence makes him inaccessible. He is embodied in the blank spaces between the reiterated questions. If God is absence, prayer is despair; in the conclusive part of the poem, this mood is sealed by the discarding of the choral address in favor of a third-person statement which weighs all of man's works, his prideful creations, to find them wanting. Man thinks he can "broaden his possessions" while "from his feverish hands/ Boundaries only issue, endlessly." Man

> clinging on the void
> To his own cobweb,
> Fears nothing, seduces nothing
> But his own cry.

Man

> repairs the waste by raising tombs,
> And to conceive you, O Eternal,
> He has but blasphemies.

"La Pietà" is one of the crucial statements in twentieth-century poetry, a religious probing of our culture, though in no merely devotional key. The biblical eloquence is sustained by much dazzling imagery and even more by the solemn cadence which the alternation of agonizing questions with silence engenders. The language is blunt, rugged, reminiscent of Jacopone da Todi's mediaeval asperity. The rest of the "Hymns" stick to this keynote, with "Caino" ("Cain"), "La preghiera" ("The Prayer"), and "Dannazione" ("Damnation") likewise claiming earnest attention, and a further sequence titled "La morte meditata" ("Meditations on Death") providing the logical conclusion. Man stands in judgment on himself; the Bible, not pagan mythology, is now his text, prayer and anguish supersede the earlier sorcery. Cain is the inner self of us all. Radical questions arise, to remain unanswered:

Come il sasso aspro del vulcano,
Come il logoro sasso del torrente,
Come la notte sola e nuda,
Anima da fionda e da terrori
Perché non ti raccatta
La mano ferma del Signore?

(Like the sharp boulder of volcanoes,
Like the gnawed pebble of the torrent,
Like night itself alone and bare,
O soul fit for the slingshot and for terrors
Why aren't you picked up
By the firm hand of the Lord?)

These lines are from "Dannazione." In "The Rivers," when war was all around but not within him, the poet had envisaged his own elemental self as a stone gently polished by the Isonzo's friendly waters into harmonious form: time was no enemy, nor were the elements. Here, the same key image recurs, with inverted value. The world of time and of the elements is infernally threatening, the soul is at their mercy and can hope for safety only from the unresponsive Transcendent. War is within, not without: a worse predicament by far for the poet who had said "My torture/is when/I don't believe myself/in harmony." There is no question, now, of finding peace as "a docile fiber/of the universe."

As happens, this malaise was prophetic of the new apocalyptic conflict that went on smouldering for some time in men's troubled souls during the uneasy lull between the two wars, and the very imagery and tone of "Damnation" may supply a cue to the most impressive poem of *Il Dolore*, the fruit of bereavement in Brazil and of return to war-tortured Italy. "Tu Ti Spezzasti" ("You Shattered") commemorates the poet's son, struck down by premature death overseas, in a savage cosmic setting where chaos still lurks:

I molti, immani, sparsi, grigi sassi
Frementi ancora alle segrete fionde
Di originarie fiamme soffocate
Od ai terrori di fiumane vergini
Ruinanti in implacabili carezze,
—Sopra l'abbaglio della sabbia rigidi
In un vuoto orizzonte, non rammenti?

(The many, immense, sparse, gray boulders
Still quivering from the secret slingshots
Of original suffocated fires
Or at the terrors of virgin torrents
Rushing down with implacable caresses,
—Stiffly standing over the dazzle of the sand
In an empty horizon, don't you remember?)

The human disorder of war did not manage to taint the cosmic elements in *L'Allegria.* Here instead, the universe itself, far from being a peaceful haven, is the creation of demonic violence: nature is desert and jungle juxtaposed, and the very intricacy of syntax in the rush of clauses that makes up most of the massive first section of the poem mirrors a choking pain. Then, at the end of Section I, the elf-like child nimbly appears, an incongruous manifestation of grace in the midst of all this barbarous terror. Section II shows him as an angelic creature who "raised" his "arms like wings," always dancing. The voice has now moved from the initial exasperation to a serene register, and the convolutions of Section I have relaxed into the simple, short utterance which of itself suggests the momentary presence of peace. But nature is cursed, and Section III, in compressed form, renews the strain of the outset: the child was a "happy grace" foreign to this savage world, and therefore doomed to succumb to its "hardened blindness"; he was a

troppo umano lampo per l'empio,
Selvoso, accanito, ronzante
Ruggito del sole ignudo.

(too human gleam of light for the impious,
Shaggy, relentless, whirring
Roar of the naked sun.)

The powerful images, climaxing at the end in paroxystic synaesthesia, come in supporting pulses of panting rhythm, which in turn echoes the staccato effect of the very first line. Unlike the preceding sequence ("Giorno per giorno, "Day by day"), which tells the sorrow of personal loss on the level of private memory, this visionary outburst, spiraling through a musical alternation of andante mosso and largo, crescendo and diminuendo, takes on mythic proportions to depict a satanic world to which love, innocence, and grace are fleeting visitors at best. Our understanding of the poem will deepen further if we read it against the background of Leopardi's "A Silvia," on whose rhetorical structure it is freely patterned, for Leopardi too begins by asking a beloved young dead one if she remembers her short happy days on earth, and he likewise concludes on a note of despairing accusation of Nature, after envisaging in Silvia the grace and promise of which young life is capable.

Nothing else in *Il Dolore* equals this peak of measured energy, yet the ensuing poems, written in the shadow of the German occupation ("*Roma occupata*"), are far from anticlimactic. They complement the masterpiece by balancing personal grief with communal grief, the tragedy of one man with the tragedy of a whole people, and once again the collection of verse coheres in a book which demands to be read as such and not just for the sake of whatever isolated successes may be culled from its pages. Prayer and lament set the tone; Rome comes to life as a city, indeed as the scene and epitome of civilization itself, which is now in danger, and the poet in the threatened city shares the pain of his people. Though the rhetoric may occasionally become overly explicit, one consistently feels that Rome, and by the same token everything Italy is and stands for, has never been so much the poet's home. Now he really inhabits the city, and it is *his* city, as the land is his—in suffering, *Dolore*. Thus the last piece, "Terra," aptly seals the book, no matter what objections can be raised against the stylistic involution that mars it if we consider it as an independent poem. Like *Sentimento del Tempo*, the volume has a binary structure in which the second part thematically balances the first and represents a progression of experience beyond the climax reached there. Part I is exile and the memory of exile, Part II the return to the Promised Land.

But the Promised Land is more than just a city or an ancestral country; it is civilization itself, and as such it provides an antiphon to the devastations unleashed by tropical Nature. "Defunti su Montagne" ("The Dead on Mountains") implicitly answers the stoic resignation of "You Shattered." In the "Brazilian" piece savage Nature inexorably destroyed innocent grace (personified in the poet's child), but in the "Roman" piece a hope glimmers in the very midst of despair. This hope rises for the poet from a contemplation of Masaccio's Crucifixion in the church of San Clemente, where he reads the story of so many crucifixions brutally re-enacted by contemporary man, yet by the same token the power of Art and Form over barbarism, and the message of human redemption all this sorrow will yield. Here, in war-torn Europe, the barbarism elsewhere displayed by a ravenous Nature has found an even more dreadful expression in human violence; but chaos will not prevail in the end. This answers also the excruciating doubts of "La Pietà," for art no longer seems utter vanity, incarnating as it does man's saving will to form in the face of destruction. If the second part of *Sentimento del Tempo* sounded like a rejection of all human endeavor, after the stern fashion of the Book of Ecclesiastes, here instead the religious appeal is in humanistic vein, and God is addressed as "Genitrice mente," (Engendering Mind), in the style of Neoplatonic Renaissance thinkers who saw in God an inspiring source of creativity rather than an inaccessible judge.

After *Il Dolore*, *La Terra Promessa* (1950) embarks on a further consummation of experience and sets the tone for most of the poetry to come in Ungaretti's second postwar phase. The title, as we saw, brings to fruition his central myth, but the Promised Land, the place of fulfillment, is only glimpsed in intimations or lost. Aeneas' "choruses," which should be part of the title sequence if the author followed the *Aeneid*'s cue more closely, were still in inchoate form at the time of publication and therefore left out. This matters, for Aeneas, of the personae introduced into the sequence, was the only one to set foot on his Promised Land of Italy after the various wanderings Vergil recounts. The others–forsaken Dido and ill-starred Palinurus–were left behind by Aeneas, the former through an act of his will, the latter through accident as a further toll the gods imposed on the Trojan rovers. Thus the theme is one of utter loss, as if to make ironic the title itself. Dido sings in nineteen "choruses" her story of love attained and lost; memory rehearses the moments of irrevocable happiness, then the cruel disappearance and the ravages thereby inflicted on her soul, until she sees her moral image in the blighted landscape of No. XVIII, and, with the desolate resignation of laconic No. XIX, she seals her fate. The loss of love being to her one and the same thing with the loss of youth, her vicissitudes reflect the torment of aging, and the poet himself obliquely looms behind his articulate persona who, on the other hand, owes some of her traits to Racine's *Phaedra*, one of the works that occupied Ungaretti as a translator after World War II. He tells us in the foreword that Dido's autumnal figure represents also the decline of a civilization. Whether the reader is or is not inclined to follow these allegorical pointers, the fact remains that Dido's voice lives through the many modulations of bitter or enchanted recall, present distraction, wistful contemplation, and final renunciation, as one of the valid expressions of the experience of personal decline. It is a voice skillfully passing from the immediacy of "cry of love, cry of shame" (No. III) to the involved Petrarchan elaborateness of much more oblique utterances, both mobility and elegance of style fitting the poetical mask, a mask so different from Vergil's Dido yet no less passionately dignified, even to the point where she drinks her bitter cup to the dregs of inner degradation.

In the two very formal compositions which encase Dido's sequence, Ungaretti brings his Petrarchan experience to a complete consummation. Their stately style, marked by abstract vocabulary, complexity of construction, and closed meter, fits their respective themes; it also acts as a foil to the more animated ejaculations and meditations of Dido. In the first piece, which precedes Dido's sequence, the poet sings his own descent into the inner abyss of oblivion and nothingness (the death of the senses) and his subsequent rise to another sphere of being at the call of the Platonic "first image" which still glimmers, in Promised-Land fashion, through the world of inconstancy. Thus he offsets by dedication to vision and form the inevitable loss whose degrading impact Dido can only stop by dying. This introductory "canzone" ties in with the symmetrical sestina of Palinurus, who symbolizes questing man overtaken by the twin delusions of dream and feverish action, and by them doomed. He has become stone, nothing else is left of his struggle with the untrustworthy waters: "Così divenni furia non mortale," ("thus I became non-mortal fury"). He personifies the fate of our Faustian civilization as well as the process whereby art immobilizes life into a perennial form. Both he and the poet keep striving for the Promised Land to the very last; Palinurus is the defeated man of action, the poet is the man of contemplation (the only one with a chance left), and Dido, the defeated creature of passion. Together, they make up man's sundered inner trinity.

Il Taccuino del Vecchio (*Notebook of an Old Man*), appearing ten years after, prolongs *La Terra Promessa* in theme and form, even to the extent of incorporating some of the "choruses" originally assigned to Aeneas (they are now collectively designated as "Last Choruses for the Promised Land"). In between, *Un Grido e Paesaggi* (*A Cry and Landscapes*) comes in 1952 as a throwback to the less elaborate stages of Ungaretti's career. Its mainstay is a long narrative piece called "Monologhetto" ("Little Monologue") which stems from the vivid prose of *The Desert and After*. It seems somehow a new version of "The Rivers": a retelling of the writer's pilgrimages in the light of the meaning they can yield in retrospect. Yet the recapitulating voice has a very different tone, it unwinds from the spool of memory with an unremitting urgency of its own which the 1916 poem, with its suspended images and unpunctuated free stanzas, never attains. "I Fiumi" was a poem of wonder flowing in mythic time; "Monologhetto" is closer to historical time and narrative prose, and contains a critique of experience the ecstatic earlier poem did not envisage. "The Rivers" was essentially a celebration of fulfillment, a finding of the self in a reliable universe, while "Monologhetto" is an ironic facing of disenchantment: "Poets, O poets, we have donned/All the masks;/But one is only one's own self . . ."

This mask motif, oddly reminiscent of Pound's gesture toward the end of *Pisan Cantos* ("Pull down thy vanity . . ."), thematically springs from the occasion of the poem, which has to do with the author's birthday in the month of February and thus with the Carnival season. Carnival in Corsica, carnival in Brazil, and in a way, carnival in Egypt (the Shi'ite Moslem festival of moon amulets) form a set of recurrent celebrations of the equivocal through the several places the poet has visited in the course of a long life, until the eerie meaning of all masquerades comes home to him, the seeker of truth. Toward the end of the reminiscence, the nightmarish prophecies of a hallucinated Arab woman are deflated by the peasant commonsense wisdom of the poet's mother; masks, dreams, irrational visions, are all equivocations man should learn to discard, as the autobiographical persona has done. Better face the emptiness of winter, of old age, of disenchantment, and mind the biblical warning "Thou art dust . . ." Dreams are for children; yet, the poem asks, why does childhood so suddenly become a fading memory? The conclusion is

> Nothing, nothing else is there on this earth
> But a glimmer of truth
> And the nothingness of dust,
> Even if, in incorrigible madness,
> Toward the lightning splendor of mirages
> Living man, deep down and in his gestures
> Forever seems to tend.

Experience is the progressive exorcism of illusion, yet will bare truth be enough? The Leopardian dilemma runs through this poetical monologue just as it does through Ungaretti's entire career, an ever-resumed journey toward the ever-changing Promised Land. For, if man's choice is between the desert and a mirage, as some of the *Notebook of an Old Man* intimates, there is no hope. Ungaretti's undeniable religious inspiration is of the stern, not of the facile consolatory variety. From his loss he draws his sustenance, and thus, rather than give up, he pursues his quest:

> We flee toward a goal:
> Who will ever know it?
>
> Not of Ithaca do we dream
> Lost in sea wanderings,
> But our aim goes to Sinai over sands . . .
>
> (T d V, 4)

"Non d'Itaca si sogna," for you can't go home again, yet even Sinai is not a definitive goal, for

> if [our life on earth] is cut short on top of Sinai,
> The law is renewed for those who are left,
> Illusion will rage again.

Poet, seer, thinker, are one and the same thing, priests of truth, but this hard-won truth must be shared, or else life will have been in vain. Here Ungaretti seems to echo that passage of Plato's *Republic* where the philosopher liberated from the shadow-knowledge of the cave is admonished not to turn his back forever on his former fellow inmates.

And Ungaretti has kept faith with this generous asceticism. As a poet, he has (to say it with Pound's Propertius) "kept his erasers in order." Emulating Mallarmé's, Petrarch's, or Leopardi's purity never meant for him what it would have meant for the lord of Axel's castle; on the contrary, he has insisted on sharing his message and his love of form with other men, contact being provided by "joy," by "sorrow," and by the very uncertainties of the human condition. As a consequence, he is one of very few modern writers who pursued both a goal of "absolute poetry" and a breakthrough to dramatic immediacy and historical relevance. A deep faith, with the strength to question everything one has been and done; a language repossessed; a word spoken in time, but for all time. Nomad Ungaretti has indeed found his home in the Italian language, though as civilized man he is at home in so much of the world, and as believer he must keep looking through the sands of time for the Promised Land which cannot be finally granted to the living.

By way of postscript I append, in my translation, three exemplary poems, respectively from *L'Allegria*, *Sentimento del Tempo*, and *Il Taccuino del Vecchio*, to which reference has been made in the text.

Half Asleep (1916)

I assist the violated night

The air is riddled
like a lace
by the gunshots
of men
recoiling
in the trenches
as snails in their shells

It sounds as if
a panting
swarm of stonecutters
were pounding the lava
cobblestones
of my streets
and I listen
unseeing
half asleep

Cain (1928)

He runs over the fabled sands
And swift is his foot.

O shepherd of wolves,
You have the teeth of the brief light
That penetrates our days.

Terrors, jumps,
Groans of forests, the hand
Which shatters old oaks at one stroke,

You are made in the image of our heart.

And when the hour turns to deepest darkness
Are you the body frolicking
Among the spellbound trees?

And while I burst with yearning,
Time changes, shadowy you roam,
With my own step you run from me.

Oh, to sleep, like a spring in the shade!

When morning is still hidden,
You would be welcomed, soul,
By a restful wave.

O soul, shall I calm you ever?

Ever see through the night of my blood?

Unwelcome offspring of futility,
Memory, unrelenting memory,
Is there no wind to blow away
The clouds of your dust?

My eyes would become innocent again,
I should see the eternal Spring

And, new at long last,
O memory, you would be honest.

Last Choruses for the Promised Land—No. 24 (1959)

Let the kite clutch me in his blue talons
And, at the climax of the sun,
Drop me in the sand
To feed the ravens' hunger.

No longer shall I carry the mud's burden,
Fire will have purified me,
And the croaking beaks,
And the jackals' sharp smelling fangs.

Then the bedouin will show,
Probing the sand
With his knowledgeable stick,
A heap of whitest bones.

SELECTED BIBLIOGRAPHY

NOTE: *For a full bibliography of Ungaretti's verse and prose writings up to 1961, inclusive of his uncollected articles in the daily or periodical press, see the appendixes of Luciano Rebay's monograph listed below. For a critical bibliography of essays and reviews concerning Ungaretti's work from 1917 to 1958, see Renzo Frattarolo's article in the special 1958 issue of* Letteratura *(pp. 363–71), listed below; additional contributions are reported in Rebay's book and in Anceschi and Antonielli's anthology of modern Italian poetry,* Lirica del Novecento *(Florence, 1953, 1963). Further up-to-date information is to be found in such periodicals as* Rassegna della letteratura italiana *and* Libri e Riviste d'Italia, *as well as in PMLA's annual bibliographical issue. All or most of the relevant publications are available in the best American libraries, such as Harvard's Widener Library, New York Public Library, Yale University Library, Columbia University Library, Princeton Library, and others. It should be kept in mind that good modern Italian collections are scattered throughout the North American continent in the libraries of such universities as Toronto, the University of Michigan, Indiana University, UCLA at Berkeley and Los Angeles, Bryn Mawr, Rutgers, the University of North Carolina at Chapel Hill, the University of Chicago, and others. A useful collection of current periodicals and tape recordings is available at the Istituto Italiano di Cultura in New York.*

PRINCIPAL WORKS OF GIUSEPPE UNGARETTI

Vita d'un Uomo. Milan, 1942 to present. (This is the general title of his collected volumes of verse and prose, twelve so far, which have been issued or reissued by Mondadori Publishers of Milan. Separate titles follow.)

L'Allegria. (Originally published as Allegria di Naufragi, Florence, 1919. An edition including the earlier volume *Il Porto Sepolto.* Udine, 1916.)

Sentimento del Tempo. With an introductory essay by Alfredo Gargiulo. (Originally published in Florence and in Rome, 1933.)

Poesie Disperse. With the variants of all the poems in *L'Allegria* and *Sentimento del Tempo*, and a critical study by Giuseppe de Robertis. 1945.

40 Sonetti di Shakespeare tradotti. 1946.

Il Dolore. 1947.

Da Góngora e da Mallarmé (translations). 1948.

La Terra Promessa. With a critical study by Leone Piccioni. 1950.
Fedra di Jean Racine. 1950.
Un Grido e Paesaggi. With a study by Piero Bigongiari. 1952, 1954.
Il Taccuino del Vecchio. 1960. (A de luxe edition, now out of print, includes testimonials by many famous foreign writers, from Paulhan to Eliot.)
Il Deserto e Dopo. 1961.
Visioni di William Blake (translations). With facsimiles of Blake's engravings, and extensive notes by Mario Diacono. 1965.

TRANSLATIONS OF UNGARETTI'S WORKS

La Guerre. Une poésie de Giuseppe Ungaretti. Paris, 1919. (Verse partly self-translated and partly written originally in French by the author.)
Les Cinq Livres. Texte français établi par l'auteur et Jean Lescure. Paris, 1954.
The Promised Land and Other Poems. Sergio Pacifici, ed. New York, 1957.
Life of a Man. A version with introduction by Allen Mandelbaum. London, Milan, and New York, 1958.
The Penguin Book of Italian Verse. George Kay, ed. and tr. 1958, 1965.
El Dolor, Vintila Horia, tr. Madrid, 1958.
Suplemento Literário de "O Estado de São Paulo," 491 (August 20, 1966), 1. Brazilian translations ("Poemas de Ungaretti") by Ecléa Bosi and I. Bettarello. Articles by Alfredo Bosi ("A Lição de Ungaretti") and Antonio Candido ("Ungaretti em São Paulo").
Giuseppe Ungaretti tradotto da Pierre Jean Jouve. Milan, 1960.
Lowell, Robert. Imitations. New York, 1961.
Gedichte, Italienisch und deutsch. Uebertragung und Nachwort von Ingeborg Bachmann. Frankfurt am Main, 1961.
Antología de la Poesía Italiana, Selección, Versión y Prólogo de Manuel Durán. Mexico, 1961.
Translations (French) from *Il Taccuino del Vecchio*, by Francis Ponge, Facsimile edition with Ungaretti's texts and variants. Milan, Guido Le Noci publ., 1963.
Italian Poetry, ed. Sonia Raiziss and Alfredo de Palchi, in: Modern European Poetry, ed. Willis Barnstone. Bantam Classics DC289, 1966.
Italian Sampler, an Anthology of Italian Verse, tr. by Thomas G. Bergin. Montreal, 1964.

Anceschi, Luciano. Le Poetiche del Novecento. Milan, 1962.
Bigongiari, Piero. Poesia Italiana del Novecento. Milan, 1960.
Bo, Carlo. Otto Studi. Florence, 1940.
Cambon, Glauco. "Ungaretti's Poetry from Evocation to Invocation," *Italian Quarterly*, V–VI (1962), 97–105.
Cavalli, Gigi. Ungaretti. Milan, 1958.
Cecchetti, Giovanni. "Giuseppe Ungaretti," *Italica*, XXVI, 4 (December 1949), 269–79.
Contini, Gianfranco. Esercizi di lettura sopra autori contemporanei. Florence, 1947.
Crémieux, Benjamin. Panorama de la littérature italienne contemporaine. Paris, 1928.
De Campos, Haroldo. "Ungaretti e a poética do fragmento," *Correio da Manhã*. Rio de Janeiro, May 28, 1967.
———. "Ungaretti e a vanguarda," *Suplemento Literário de "O Estado de São Paulo,"* 494 (August 10, 1966), 3. With translation of one of Ungaretti's poems into Brazilian.
De Nardis, Luigi. Mallarmé in Italia. Milan, 1957.
De Robertis, Giuseppe. Scrittori del Novecento. Florence, 1946.
Falqui, Enrico. Pezze d'appoggio antiche e nuove. Appunti sulla letteratura italiana contemporanea. Rome, 1951.
Flora, Francesco. La poesia ermetica. Bari, 1936.
Friedrich, Hugo. Die Struktur der modernen Lyrik. Hamburg, 1956.
Gargiulo, Alfredo. Letteratura italiana del Novecento. Florence, 1943.
Gutia, Joan. Linguaggio di Ungaretti. Florence, 1959.
Hinterhauser, Hans. Moderne Italienische Lyrik. Goettingen, 1964.
Letteratura 35–36 (Rome, September–December 1958. Special issue for Ungaretti's seventieth birthday, comprising several studies, by Ferrata, Piccioni, Paci, De Robertis, Schiaffini, Barberi-Squarotti, Macrì, Bocelli, Apollonio, Bigongiari, Spagnoletti, Cecchi, Sanguineti, Mariani, and others.
Pacifici, Sergio. A Guide to Contemporary Italian Literature. Meridian Books, 1962.
Pento, Bortolo. Poesia Contemporanea. Milan, 1964.
Petrucciani, Mario. La poetica dell'ermetismo italiano. Turin, 1955.
Poggioli, Renato. "Contemporary Italian Poetry," *Voices*, 128, Winter 1947.
Pozzi, Gianni. La poesia italiana del Novecento. Turin, 1965.

Ragusa, Olga. Mallarmé in Italy, Literary Influence and Critical Response. New York, 1957.
Rebay, Luciano. Le origini della poesia di Ungaretti. Rome, 1962.
Sempoux, André. "Le premier Ungaretti et la France," *Revue de Littérature Comparée*, XXXVII, 3 (July–September 1963), 360–67.
Vallone, Aldo. Aspetti della poesia italiana contemporanea. Pisa, 1960.
Williamson, Edward. "Contemporary Italian Poetry," *Poetry*, LXXIX, 3 (December 1951), 159–81.

AUTHOR'S NOTE. At this writing (1967) the Paris magazine *L'Herne* is preparing a special issue on Ungaretti under the editorship of Piero Sanavio.

Date Due
